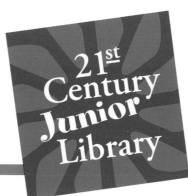

21st Century Junior Library

Saber-Toothed Cat

by Jennifer Zeiger

CHERRY LAKE PUBLISHING * ANN ARBOR, MICHIGAN

CHERRY LAKE
Publishing

Published in the United States of America by Cherry Lake Publishing
Ann Arbor, Michigan
www.cherrylakepublishing.com

Content Adviser: Gregory M. Erickson, PhD, Paleontologist, Department of Biological Science,
Florida State University, Tallahassee, Florida

Reading Adviser: Marla Conn, Read With Me Now

Photo Credits: Cover top, © Kostyantyn Ivanyshen/Shutterstock.com; cover bottom and page 12,
© TsuneoMP/Shutterstock.com; page 4, © Catmando/Shutterstock.com; page 6, © Ozja/Shutter-
stock.com; page 8, © iStockphoto.com/WLDavies; page 10, © AP Photo/Damian Dovarganes;
page 14, © National Geographic Image Collection/Alamy; page 16, © Stocktrek Images, Inc./Alamy;
page 18, © mikeledray/Shutterstock.com; page 20, © AP Photo/The Fresno Bee, Mark Crosse.

LIBRARY OF CONGRESS CATALOGING-IN-PUBLICATION DATA
Zeiger, Jennifer, author.
  Saber-toothed cat / by Jennifer Zeiger.
     pages cm.—(Dinosaurs) (21st century junior library)
  Summary: "Learn all about the ancient animals known as saber-toothed cats, from what they ate to
how they are related to today's cats."—Provided by publisher.
  Audience: K to grade 3
  Includes bibliographical references and index.
  ISBN 978-1-63362-386-6 (lib. bdg.)—ISBN 978-1-63362-414-6 (pbk.)—
ISBN 978-1-63362-442-9 (pdf)—ISBN 978-1-63362-470-2 (e-book)
  1. Saber-toothed tigers—Juvenile literature. 2. Extinct mammals—Juvenile literature. [1. Prehistoric
animals.] I. Title.
QE882.C15Z45 2016
569.74—dc23   2014045659

Cherry Lake Publishing would like to acknowledge the work of
The Partnership for 21st Century Skills.
Please visit www.p21.org for more information.

Printed in the United States of America
Corporate Graphics
July 2015

CONTENTS

A saber-toothed cat watches for its next meal.

What Was a Saber-Toothed Cat?

Imagine an ancient **grassland**. A large cat crouches in the long grass. It is covered in fur, just like cats today. It has sharp claws and strong legs. Two long **canine teeth** stick out from its mouth. These teeth give the cat its name. It is a saber-toothed cat! A saber is a long, curved sword.

Many saber-toothed cats lived where the
weather could become very cold.

Saber-toothed cats were once found around the world. Europe, Asia, Africa, and North and South America had saber-toothed cats. These animals lived between 38 million and 10,000 years ago. Some saber-toothed cats met early humans. None of these cats are alive today, though. They are **extinct**.

Ask Questions!

There are many reasons a plant or animal might go extinct. Can you think of any? Talk to a teacher, librarian, parent, or other trusted adult. Ask what they know about it. Have any plants or animals gone extinct while you were alive?

Some saber-toothed cats were about as big as today's lions.

What Did a Saber-Toothed Cat Look Like?

In many ways, saber-toothed cats looked like today's lions or tigers. They were covered in fur and walked on four legs. Their paws were large. Each paw had sharp claws. The claws only came out when they were needed. Some saber-toothed cats had long tails. Others had almost no tail at all.

The tooth on the left belonged to a baby
saber-toothed cat. The one on the right
belonged to an adult.

What do you notice first about a saber-toothed cat? Probably its two canine teeth! These teeth could be as long as 8 inches (20 centimeters)! They stuck out even when the cat closed its mouth. The cat had to open its mouth very wide to use these teeth.

Think!

Other animals have really long teeth, too. Some of these animals were around thousands or millions of years ago. Others are alive today! Can you think of any? Hint: Tusks are a type of tooth.

Saber-toothed cats used their strong legs to pounce
on the animals they hunted.

Some saber-toothed cats had short legs. These cats were heavy and strong. They were not fast, but they were good at jumping. Other saber-toothed cats were taller. They had longer, thinner legs. This helped them run fast.

Large ground sloths were sometimes a
saber-toothed cat's meal.

How Did a Saber-Toothed Cat Live?

Just like cats today, saber-toothed cats ate meat. They were **predators**. They usually hunted animals that were much larger than they were. These animals included horses and bison. Some saber-toothed cats may even have hunted humans.

15

Saber-toothed cats may have worked together,
much like today's wolves or lions.

Experts believe that some saber-toothed cats lived in **packs**. They may have cared for sick, injured, or old pack members. They also hunted together. This made it easier to take down very large animals.

Modern cats do not usually live in packs. Lions are the only cats today that live in groups.

A saber-toothed cat's large teeth were
fearsome weapons.

Teeth, claws, and strength made saber-toothed cats great hunters. But these features were also used for defense. Dire wolves, American lions, and other ancient predators sometimes attacked. Humans may have attacked saber-toothed cats, too. The cats also fought one another over food, **territory**, and **mates**.

The La Brea Tar Pits contain fossils of saber-toothed cats, dire wolves, mastodons, and many other ancient animals.

How do we know about saber-toothed cats? Experts study **fossils**. Fossils give clues about how an animal lived. People have found thousands of saber-toothed cat fossils. Many of them were discovered in California's La Brea Tar Pits. More fossils are found all the time. Each new fossil provides a new clue. What might experts discover next?

GLOSSARY

canine teeth (KAY-nine TEETH) the long, pointed teeth near the front of an animal's lower and upper jaws

extinct (ek-STINGKT) describing a type of plant or animal that has completely died out

fossils (FAH-suhlz) the preserved remains of living things from thousands or millions of years ago

grassland (GRAS-land) a large, open area of grass

mates (MAYTS) animals that produce young together

packs (PAKS) groups of animals living as a unit

predators (PRED-uh-turz) animals that live by hunting other animals for food

territory (TER-i-tor-ee) an area of land claimed by an animal

FIND OUT MORE

BOOKS

O'Brien, Patrick. *Sabertooth*. New York: Henry Holt and Co., 2008.

Thomson, Sarah L. *Ancient Animals: Saber-Toothed Cat*. Watertown, MA: Charlesbridge, 2014.

WEB SITES

BBC Nature—Prehistoric Life: Smilodon
www.bbc.co.uk/nature/life/Smilodon
Watch videos and learn about one of the most famous types of saber-toothed cats, the *Smilodon*.

Page Museum at the La Brea Tar Pits
www.tarpits.org
Want to learn more about the La Brea Tar Pits? This Web site offers information on the area's history and importance to prehistoric studies.

INDEX

ABOUT THE AUTHOR

Jennifer Zeiger lives in Chicago, Illinois. She writes and edits children's books on all sorts of topics.